THE POCKET
HORROR MOVIES

Published in 2025
by Gemini Books
Part of Gemini Books Group

Based in Woodbridge and London

Marine House, Tide Mill Way,
Woodbridge, Suffolk IP12 1AP
United Kingdom

www.geminibooks.com

Text and Design © 2025 Gemini Adult Books Ltd

Text by Roland Hall
Cover illustration by Natalie Floss

ISBN 978-1-80247-300-1

All rights reserved. No part of this publication may be reproduced in any form or by any means – electronic, mechanical, photocopying, recording or otherwise – or stored in any retrieval system of any nature without prior written permission from the copyright holders.

A CIP catalogue record for this book is available
from the British Library.

Disclaimer: The book is a guidebook purely for information and entertainment purposes only. All trademarks, individual and company names, brand names, registered names, quotations, celebrity names, logos, dialogues and catchphrases used or cited in this book are the property of their respective owners. The publisher does not assume and hereby disclaim any liability to any party for any loss, damage or disruption caused by errors or omissions, whether such errors or omissions result from negligence, accident, or any other cause. This book is an unofficial and unauthorized publication by Gemini Adult Books Ltd and has not been licensed, approved, sponsored or endorsed by any person or entity.

Manufacturer's EU Representative: Eurolink Compliance Limited,
25 Herbert Place, Dublin, D02 AY86, Republic of Ireland.
admin@eurolink-europe.ie

Printed in China

10 9 8 7 6 5 4 3 2 1

Picture Credits: Alamy Stock Photo: Everett Collection Inc 4; TCD/Prod. DB 6; Moviestore Collection Ltd 16; ScreenProd / Photononstop 118. Shutterstock: Anastasiia Hevko 120, 121, 124, 125, 127.

THE POCKET

HORROR MOVIES

G:

CONTENTS

Introduction 6

50 Must-see Horror Movies 16

Directors' Cut 118

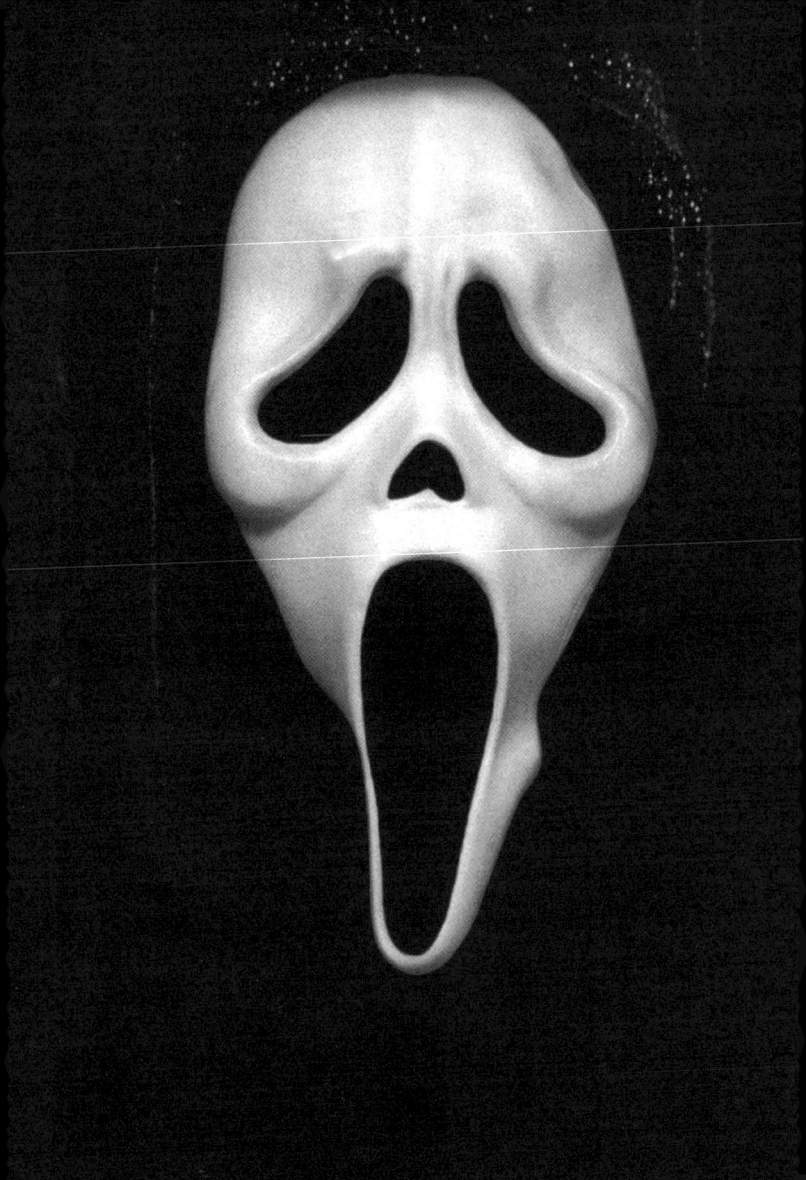

INTRODUCTION

Horror in the movies comes in all shapes and sizes. It can be gooey, slimy and misty or solid, pointed and blunt. It can be subtle, careful and delicate or often brutal, graphic and gruesome. It can jump out from behind a wall or be hidden under a bed. It can be long and drawn out or over in a flash. It can make you laugh, cry and scream. So there's something for everyone.

Humankind loves stories, and we have a taste for scary ones. We take pleasure in frightening each other in the name of fun – but deep down, we are all scared of something.

HORROR MOVIES

It was not long after the advent of movies that people started to make scary ones. This should come as no surprise, for scary books had long been in print and selling very well. Popular children's stories often feature a monster. Something or someone different, something to be afraid of, especially if you did not behave yourself. And what are adults but grown-up children? So it is little surprise that, for a long time, the staple of the horror film was an actual monster.

INTRODUCTION

"Horror is a universal language; we're all afraid."

— John Carpenter, interview with Dave Portner, *Interview* magazine, 2015

HORROR MOVIES

"I want to have fun with horror movies."

— Sam Raimi, interview with Chris Hewitt, *Empire*, 2023

INTRODUCTION

As filmmaking techniques evolved, so did the special effects in horror films. In the early days of horror cinema, shadows, sounds and subtlety ruled, making for some disturbing viewing even then. Later, more cinematic techniques were developed to frighten the audience, the "jump scare" being the most popular.

At some point, horror became identified with gore, and we were presented with fully graphic imagery of all manner of unspeakable acts: disembowelling, tearing limb from limb and so on.

HORROR MOVIES

But it is not gory scenes and bloody violence that make the best horror films (although they do have their place). The best are ones that fill you with a sense of unease and make you check your surroundings. If you are alone, you may turn the light on. If you are in a group, you glance at your companions, just to see if they are showing signs of infection... or worse.

This book lists 50 essential movies, chosen because they are outstanding. Some are gory, some are subtle, but all of them are good and they will surely leave an impression on you, whether you like it or not...

INTRODUCTION

"Scary movies don't create fear. They release fear."

— Wes Craven, interview with Mark Kermode, the *Guardian*, 2024

HORROR MOVIES

THE SCARE FACTOR

There is a "scare factor" listed in the reviews that follow. It is simply an indicator of how disturbing the film is, solely in the author's opinion. A mark of 1 is given to an old, black-and-white movie with little violence or jeopardy, whereas a 5 indicates graphic violence, extremely disturbing themes and something likely to give you nightmares. You have been warned.

INTRODUCTION

"I hope the audience has had a good fright."

— **Stanley Kubrick on *The Shining*, in *Kubrick* by Michel Ciment, 1982**

50 MUST-SEE HORROR MOVIES

HORROR MOVIES

① Nosferatu – Eine Symphonie des Grauens (Nosferatu: A Symphony of Horror), 1922

Director: F.W. Murnau
Runtime: 63–90 mins, depending on version
Scare factor: 1/5

This silent, black-and-white film is dark and magnificent. The story is based on *Dracula* and the action takes place in Wisborg, a made-up town in Germany. Thomas Hutter is sent to Transylvania by his boss to visit a client. After a strange dinner with the mysterious Count Orlok (who tries to drink his blood!), Hutter wakes the next day with puncture marks in his neck. It doesn't get much better...

Dripping with symbolism, richly multi-themed (it was filmed between two world wars), *Nosferatu* is a brilliantly realized movie that stands up well to modern viewing. Although not too frightening by today's standards, you won't sleep better after a late-night viewing.

50 MUST-SEE HORROR MOVIES

"Your wife has such a beautiful neck."

— Count Orlock

HORROR MOVIES

"In the name of God, now I know what it feels like to be God!"

— Henry Frankenstein

② Frankenstein, 1931
Director: James Whale
Runtime: 70+- mins, depending on version
Scare factor: 2/5

Is it science fiction? (Yes). Is it horror? (Yes). Is it a creepy classic? Hell yes. Based on the Gothic literary masterpiece *Frankenstein; or, The Modern Prometheus* by Mary Shelley, this adaptation features Boris Karloff in the role that defined what the "Monster" would resemble for evermore.

A slimmed down version of the book's story (see *Mary Shelley's Frankenstein* by Kenneth Branagh for a (slightly) more faithful adaptation), Frankenstein and his assistant Fritz build a creature out of used body parts and the brain of a criminal. What could possibly go wrong? This movie's got it all, and still manages to ask some pertinent questions on what makes a monster, and on madness and genius.

HORROR MOVIES

③ Psycho, 1960
Director: Alfred Hitchcock
Runtime: 109 mins
Scare factor: 3/5

Psycho regularly tops "best movie" lists as well as "best horror movie" lists, and when you've seen it you'll know why. Hugely influential, *Psycho* was utterly original then and is often referred to as Hitchcock's greatest movie.

Marion Crane (Janet Leigh) steals money from her employer and sets off on the drive to join her boyfriend. Caught by foul weather, she stops at the (now infamous) Bates Motel where she meets the gentle Norman (Anthony Perkins), who runs the place under his dominant mother's beady eye... Much of the action takes place after the focus of the story switches to boyfriend Sam. Violent, scary and shocking, *Psycho* is a masterpiece.

50 MUST-SEE HORROR MOVIES

"Well, a boy's best friend is his mother."

— Norman Bates

HORROR MOVIES

④ Repulsion, 1965
Director: Roman Polanski
Runtime: 105 mins
Scare factor: 4/5

An underrated psychological horror classic, *Repulsion* is the highly original, disturbing tale of a young woman's descent into madness. Carole Ledoux (Catherine Deneuve) lives in London with her sister and experiences various nightmares and hallucinations. She has a boyfriend, as does her sister, but everyday interactions become increasingly difficult as she becomes further distanced from reality.

Some great cinematic techniques are used, and some of the special effects went on to become staples in horror movies down the years (hands in the walls, mirror-jump cuts). The movie is genuinely unsettling.

50 MUST-SEE HORROR MOVIES

"There's no need to be alone, you know. Poor little girl. All by herself. All shaking like a little frightened animal."

— The landlord

HORROR MOVIES

"I oughtta drag you out there and feed you to those things!"

— Ben

⑤ Night of the Living Dead, 1968
Director: George A. Romero
Runtime: 96 mins
Scare factor: 3/5

If you've ever wondered where modern zombie movies came from, look no further. This bleak black-and-white, low-budget movie, where "ghouls" come to life, changed the face of horror movies for ever. The first of George A. Romero's five zombie films, any of the others are worth watching too, as budget and scope increase every time – not to mention sophistication and realism of the special effects as the undead gorge on the recently living.

Not as scary as it was nearly six decades on, but an uncomfortable watch nonetheless, *Night of the Living Dead* still – deservedly – maintains cult status and can be seen regularly on big screens.

HORROR MOVIES

⑥ Rosemary's Baby, 1968
Director: Roman Polanski
Runtime: 96 mins
Scare factor: 3/5

Rosemary's Baby is a disturbing psychological horror-thriller, where the viewer is subjected to the same anxieties and fears as the unfortunate woman of the title.

Rosemary Woodhouse (Mia Farrow) and her husband Guy (John Cassavetes) move to a new apartment block in Manhattan. It's an odd building, where creepy neighbours come and go, and Rosemary – you guessed it – becomes pregnant (itself an ugly turn of events). A book about witchcraft features, and the story arc gains clarity, but is no less disturbing.

Ruth Gordon won an Oscar for her portrayal of neighbour Minnie Castevet and the film won various other awards. It's still an unsettling experience today.

50 MUST-SEE HORROR MOVIES

"This is no dream! This is really happening!"

— Rosemary Woodhouse

HORROR MOVIES

⑦ The Exorcist, 1973
Director: William Friedkin
Runtime: 122 mins
Scare factor: 4/5

The Exorcist was nominated for the Academy Award for Best Picture in 1974 – the first horror to do so – and it did win Oscars for Best Sound and Best Screenplay Based on Material from Another Medium. Seemingly a simple tale of possession (if there could be such a thing), *The Exorcist* is a very disturbing look at faith and religious belief.

Actress Chris MacNeil (Ellen Burstyn) has a daughter, Regan (Linda Blair), who becomes possessed by a foul-mouthed demon. Most of the action takes place in the young girl's bedroom, where unspeakable acts take place as the demon wreaks havoc. The movie is still powerful, disturbing and shocking – no wonder it was banned in many countries at the time of release. It remains one of the most important movies ever made, and a cultural reference point that shows no sign of fading.

50 MUST-SEE HORROR MOVIES

"Your mother sucks cocks in Hell, Karras, you faithless slime!"

— **The demon**

HORROR MOVIES

⑧ The Wicker Man, 1973
Director: Robin Hardy
Runtime: 87–99 mins
Scare factor: 2/5

The pinnacle of folk horror and easily one of the best British horror movies ever made, *The Wicker Man* takes the viewer on an uneasy journey to a remote Scottish island, where Sergeant Neil Howie (Edward Woodward) is dispatched to investigate a young girl's disappearance. He finds all sorts of godless, chaotic behaviour, encountering the eccentric Lord Summerisle (Christopher Lee), not to mention a naked Britt Ekland hammering on his bedroom door at night.

Creepy villagers, mysterious noises and a deep sense of unease accompany Howie on his investigation. Mixing paganism, folk traditions and a thrilling mystery, *The Wicker Man* eschews explicit violence for a more cerebral tension – and succeeds brilliantly.

"The Wicker Man was the best-scripted film I ever took part in."

— Christopher Lee, in *The Wicker Man: The Official Story of the Film* by John Walsh, 2023

HORROR MOVIES

"I'm not going to get involved with two neurotic old women in a session of mumbo-jumbo."

— John Baxter

⑨ Don't Look Now, 1973
Director: Nicolas Roeg
Runtime: 110 mins
Scare factor: 2/5

Only just scraping into our list of all-time great horror films, *Don't Look Now* is more psychological thriller than traditional shocker. Don't imagine for a minute, however, that it is not genuinely disturbing – for it is. Beautifully crafted, and digging deep into the psychology of grief, belonging and humanity, the plot involves a recently bereaved couple, Laura and John Baxter (Julie Christie and Donald Sutherland), who are in Venice for work.

Creepy twin sisters offer solace and warnings. Venice is like an extra cast member, its winding alleyways and waters contributing to the sense of entrapment. It is beautifully shot and masterfully edited; a total triumph and damned unnerving to boot.

HORROR MOVIES

⑩ The Texas Chain Saw Massacre, 1974
Director: Tobe Hooper
Runtime: 83 mins
Scare factor: 4/5

It's short, it's crude and it's to the (sharp) point. *The Texas Chain Saw Massacre* (see page 4) changed the face of horror movies, taking them into deeply unpleasant territory and never looking back. A precursor to slasher movies at best and inspiration for torture porn at worst, the influence of this movie cannot be overstated.

The story is simple: teens pick up the wrong hitchhiker, visit the wrong house... and it unravels from there into a horrific, graphic tale. Explicit, nasty and shocking, the movie has so many unpleasant aspects, it's almost a relief to meet the near-dead vampire-grandad. This is the movie that gave us demented, evil Leatherface, and many people still have nightmares about him.

50 MUST-SEE HORROR MOVIES

"Well now look, you boys don't want to go messin' around some old house. Those things is dangerous. You're liable to get hurt."

— The old man

HORROR MOVIES

⑪ Carrie, 1976
Director: Brian de Palma
Runtime: 98 mins
Scare factor: 2/5

This was the first big-screen adaptation of a Stephen King novel, and it would not be the last by some distance. *Carrie* is a chilling and uncomfortable view of the teenager as outsider. Carrie's dysfunctional home life contrasts heavily with her peers, but, sadly, the bullying that ensues could happen to anyone.

Sissy Spacek is brilliant in the role of the innocent outcast Carrie, and this is one of Brian de Palma's best-realized pictures. The script is tight, the scenery perfect and the psychology is all too believable; a cautionary tale of sorts.

"If you've got a taste for terror... take Carrie to the prom."

— *Carrie* **movie poster**

HORROR MOVIES

"He wants me to stab him! He wants me to murder a child."

— Robert Thorn

⑫ The Omen, 1976
Director: Richard Donner
Runtime: 111 mins
Scare factor: 2/5

The year 1976 was a good one for movies. If you didn't find *Carrie* disturbing enough and you couldn't face *Assault on Precinct 13* or *Taxi Driver* (both of which are horrific), you could take in *The Omen*, one of the year's biggest-grossing movies.

Robert Thorn (Gregory Peck), an American diplomat, and his wife Katherine (Lee Remick) are the unwitting "recipients" of a child, Damien (the utterly unnerving Harvey Spencer Stephens), who turns out to be the Antichrist. As you would imagine, this does not make for a happy ending or indeed a happy anything.

The Omen is dark and bleak, and features some classic, powerful scenes that feature in the list of all-time horror greats (sheet-glass decapitation anyone?).

HORROR MOVIES

"You get overconfident... underestimate those suckers... and you get eaten!"

— Peter

⑬ Dawn of the Dead, 1978
Director: George A. Romero
Runtime: 119–126 mins
Scare factor: 3/5

While George A. Romero may have birthed the zombie movie with *Night of the Living Dead*, in *Dawn of the Dead* he took it to new heights, redefining the entire notion of the horror movie as he did so. There's not much of a story (natch), but what there is doubles as a criticism of governmental control, consumerism and human nature. The story's protagonists end up trapped in a shopping mall, where they must fight against zombies, outsiders... and each other.

Dawn of the Dead was the first outing for legendary special effects artist Tom Savini, and if you like your horror bloody, explicit and heavy-handed but with an underlying message, this one's for you.

HORROR MOVIES

⑭ Halloween, 1978
Director: John Carpenter
Runtime: 91 mins
Scare factor: 3/5

Two words: Michael Myers. In this movie alone, he is shot, stabbed, falls off a balcony, is stabbed again (in the eye) and still does not die. It is his first outing, but not his last by a long way.

John Carpenter made *Halloween* on a tight budget and it was a huge success, setting the tone (and quite often the storyline!) for subsequent generations of teen slasher movies, although it is probably the original and best. Myers (Tony Moran/Nick Castle) is a psychotic killer who escapes the asylum in which he is incarcerated for the brutal killing of his sister and returns to his hometown. He murders his way through the night. Teenager Laurie (Jamie Lee Curtis) and Dr Loomis (Donald Pleasence) are all that stand in his way. The masked Myers became one of the all-time great movie monsters.

50 MUST-SEE HORROR MOVIES

"You must be ready for him... If you don't, it's your funeral."

— Dr Loomis

⑮ Alien, 1979
Director: Ridley Scott
Runtime: 116 mins
Scare factor: 4/5

This is what happens when science fiction meets horror, *par excellence*. And not the Frankenstein electricity type, this is space SF at its best – and horror at its best. Ad-turned-feature director Scott provides a masterclass in tension and atmosphere, with jump scares, gore and even a cute cat.

The spaceship Nostromo is on its way to Earth when a help transmission diverts it to a nearby planet. Investigating, somebody prods an egg, a creature attaches itself to their face, and the scene is set for a sweaty, scary, anxious wander around the claustrophobic corridors of the Nostromo. A brilliant cast, an excellent director and amazing sets equal one frightening classic.

50 MUST-SEE HORROR MOVIES

"It doesn't look like an SOS... It looks like a warning."

— Ripley

HORROR MOVIES

"Look what you did to him. Look what you did to him!"

— **Pamela Voorhees**

⑯ Friday the 13th, 1980
Director: Sean S. Cunningham
Runtime: 95 mins
Scare factor: 2/5

Whether you think *Friday the 13th* is a classic teen slasher or problematic, exploitative trash, you probably won't be visiting anywhere named Camp Crystal Lake anytime soon. A simple, gory tale of uncaring teenagers punished for the actions of their predecessors, the retribution meted out to the camp counsellors is harsh – and graphic. Sex and violence dominate the movie, which for some (unexplained?) reason(s) retains its cult status with young people all over the world.

Digging deeper, the film does have more to it than might be presumed from reading a synopsis, and the back story was powerful enough to birth another timeless teen monster – Jason, who didn't even sport the trademark hockey mask until movie three.

HORROR MOVIES

⑰ The Shining, 1980
Director: Stanley Kubrick
Runtime: 119–146 mins
Scare factor: 3/5

A haunting epic, *The Shining* (see page 16) is one of the most quoted horror films ever made. Based on a Stephen King tale, this seemingly simple story of a winter caretaker (Jack Nicholson in a career-defining role) and his family (the amazing Shelley Duvall and Danny Lloyd) makes for utterly disturbing viewing. It turns out that the last caretaker killed his entire family, and that the hotel is built on an Indian burial ground.

With a soundtrack alone that'll give you a heart attack, this is an immersive horror experience like no other. An allegory on American imperialism? A treatise on racism, masculinity and sexism? Whatever it is for you, it is a genuinely outstanding movie. And never again will you suffer from writer's block... I hope.

50 MUST-SEE HORROR MOVIES

"I said, I'm not gonna hurt ya. I'm just going to bash your brains in!"

— Jack Torrance

HORROR MOVIES

⑱ The Fog, 1980
Director: John Carpenter
Runtime: 90 mins
Scare factor: 2/5

Basking in the success of *Halloween*, John Carpenter turned to the coast, where a Jamie Lee Curtis character again finds herself in trouble. Suffice it to say that the townsfolk of Antonio Bay "done wrong" to a ship and its crew as they passed by, many years previously, and on the one hundredth anniversary of that shipwreckin', revenge is in the air – in the form of a mysterious fog that drifts in from the sea. No one is safe from the fog.

It's certainly a classic, with assured direction, a stellar cast and a tight script, but it does not really reach the horror heights of *Halloween*. Don't watch it when you're on vacation on the coast, however...

50 MUST-SEE HORROR MOVIES

"Well, my gauges must be wrong. I've got a wind blowing due east. Now what kind of a fog blows against the wind?"

— Stevie Wayne

⑲ The Evil Dead, 1981
Director: Sam Raimi
Runtime: 85 mins
Scare factor: 4/5

Filmed with his friends on a rented camera, *The Evil Dead* is one odd movie. It is graphic, nasty and unnerving, and has been a huge influence on movies since. It is surprisingly artistic and quite original, possibly a result of the low-budget and homemade production techniques.

A sleeper hit on the big screens, *The Evil Dead* grew and grew, eventually making big money globally. The movie features a lot of graphic violence (including what may be the industry's only tree rape scene), and what little storyline there is gets a boost from the literary history of the *Book of the Dead*. But mainly it's a splatterfest and proud of it.

50 MUST-SEE HORROR MOVIES

"Soon all of you will be like me… And then who will lock you up in a cellar?"

— Cheryl Williams

HORROR MOVIES

"The last remaining werewolf must be destroyed. It's you, David."

— Jack

⑳ An American Werewolf in London, 1981
Director: John Landis
Runtime: 97 mins
Scare factor: 3/5

It is rare that horror and humour mix effectively, but when they do the results can be tremendous. This is one of those rare examples.

The story involves two American students, David and Jack (David Naughton and Griffin Dunne) on a trip to Europe. Jack is killed by a werewolf (although that doesn't stop him from appearing in various states of decomposition throughout the rest of the movie) and David is bitten, meaning he is cursed to change into a werewolf on a full moon. So far so bad, and as you can guess, it doesn't end well. The film is fun, revolting, technically impressive and very entertaining – although probably not one to watch when you are eating.

HORROR MOVIES

"I dunno what the hell's in there, but it's weird and pissed off, whatever it is."

— Clark

㉑ The Thing, 1982
Director: John Carpenter
Runtime: 109 mins
Scare factor: 3/5

A bloodbath on ice, *The Thing* was the next in line from godfather of modern horror John Carpenter. Fuelled by the success of *Alien* (another sci-fi/horror mashup), *The Thing* was a big-budget movie and more mainstream than Carpenter was used to. The story? The crew of an American research station investigates first the remains of a wrecked Norwegian station, then an excavation site that seems to contain an alien spacecraft. The all-male cast proceeds to destroy itself and everything around it, bit by bit.

Some have compared it to the Agatha Christie novel *And Then There Were None*, but it's more like *And Then There Was Another Explosion and Gallons of Blood*. It's extremely graphic and a good, fun exploration of the many ways a group of men can manage to kill each other.

㉒ Poltergeist, 1982
Director: Tobe Hooper
Runtime: 114 mins
Scare factor: 3/5

With a subtext that's a critique of TV, consumerism and even colonialism, *Poltergeist* works on various levels. Yes, it's a ghost story, but dig a bit deeper and it is an extremely disturbing look at contemporary America and its history. The daughter of a suburban California family disappears, "kidnapped" by ghosts who raise havoc repeatedly, terrorizing the inhabitants. It turns out that, of course, the house was built on a former cemetery...

Although directed by Tobe *Chainsaw Massacre* Hooper and "only" produced by Steven Spielberg (subsequently credited as co-director), it does feature many of the great man's hallmarks. Sadly, *Poltergeist* missed out on three Oscars – all to Steve's very own *E.T. the Extra Terrestrial*. It's a 1980s horror classic, fully deserving of its many accolades. Just don't fall asleep watching it...

50 MUST-SEE HORROR MOVIES

"They're here."

— Carol Anne Freeling

㉓ Christine, 1983
Director: John Carpenter
Runtime: 114 mins
Scare factor: 3/5

With Carpenter in the, ahem, driving seat and a Stephen King storyline, you can't really take a wrong turn with *Christine*. It's moody, it's unpleasant and it's creepy – everything you wanted from a horror film in the 1980s.

Bullied teen Arnie Cunningham buys an old car and does it up. It turns out the car has a history – and quite the jealous personality. Mayhem and murder ensue, with Arnie, ahem, driven, to even nastier acts before a final showdown. Possibly a bit dated, and a little odd by today's standards, *Christine* is nonetheless a great fun ride.

50 MUST-SEE HORROR MOVIES

"You better watch what you say about my car. She's real sensitive."

— Arnie Cunningham

HORROR MOVIES

㉔ A Nightmare on Elm Street, 1984
Director: Wes Craven
Runtime: 91 mins
Scare factor: 4/5

You'd think that American teenagers would have learned by 1984 how bad sex was for you, but nope, they keep on doing it. And what happens? The movie that shot its director to stardom is a fairly straightforward supernatural horror about torturing and killing teens. However, the many sleep/wake scenes give this one a really frantic edge, as the viewer doesn't really know what's going on, or what is real.

A huge success at the time, *A Nightmare on Elm Street* spawned multiple sequels (including one Jason/*Friday the 13th* mashup) and another of the all-time great horror-movie monsters: Freddy Krueger.

50 MUST-SEE HORROR MOVIES

"Nancy, you are going to get some sleep tonight if it kills me."

— Marge Thompson

(25) The Fly, 1986
Director: David Cronenberg
Runtime: 96 mins
Scare factor: 3/5

What do you get when you cross a man with a fly? You'll find out if you watch this one. A clue: it's sloppy, gloopy and all-round revolting, especially when in the hands of a gory director such as Cronenberg. Seth Brundle (Jeff Goldblum) is a scientist who has invented a teleportation machine. It's not perfect, however, and when he uses it on himself problems ensue, to say the least.

The Fly won the Oscar for Best Makeup in 1987 and if you watch it you'll see why. It's a pretty revolting spectacle, but stellar performances and assured direction make it a very decent movie. The tagline they could have used but (wisely) didn't: You'll believe a man can... fly?

"Be afraid. Be very afraid."

— Veronica Quaife

HORROR MOVIES

"The Cenobites gave me an experience beyond limits. Pain and pleasure, indivisible."

— Frank

㉖ Hellraiser, 1987
Director: Clive Barker
Runtime: 93 mins
Scare factor: 5/5

By the late 1980s, horror had taken a dark(er) turn and *Hellraiser*, a fantasy/horror hybrid directed by British writer Clive Barker, was at the forefront of some very unpleasant, extremely graphic manifestations. *Hellraiser* involves a mysterious puzzle box that, when solved, summons the unbelievably unpleasant "Cenobites" from Hell, who mete out unspeakable punishment on the solver; quite the fun toy. Before you know it, the box's now undead owner, Frank (Sean Chapman), is hiding in the attic and plotting the rejuvenation of his body with his brother's wife, with whom he previously had a fling. So far so good, and if it wasn't for Frank's meddling niece Kirsty (Ashley Laurence), all would go according to plan; it doesn't.

Graphic, tortuous and very disturbing, *Hellraiser* spawned many sequels, and gave the world Pinhead, one of the all-time great movie monsters.

HORROR MOVIES

㉗ Evil Dead II, 1987
Director: Sam Raimi
Runtime: 84 mins
Scare factor: 4/5

Ash is back! First encountered in *The Evil Dead*, student Ash decides to go on an outing to an abandoned cabin in the woods (do these people never learn?). That the movie ends with Ash in the Middle Ages after an almost slapstick series of grisly dismemberments tells you all you need to know.

It's an indescribable rollercoaster ride that is seemingly the product of a crazed imagination. In fact, it was the product of a few and has attracted a significant cult following in the years since its release. It's not really like any other horror film you'll ever see, but whether that's a good thing or not is up to you.

50 MUST-SEE HORROR MOVIES

"We just cut up our girlfriend with a chainsaw. Does that sound 'fine'?"

— Mirror Ash

HORROR MOVIES

㉘ Angel Heart, 1987
Director: Alan Parker
Runtime: 113 mins
Scare factor: 3/5

An underrated classic, *Angel Heart* was not universally appreciated when first released, but has since acquired cult status. The building sense of foreboding is well generated with expert director Alan Parker at the helm, and the movie retains its noir tone as investigator Harry Angel (Mickey Rourke) gets deeper into the mysterious job he has undertaken for Louis Cyphre (Robert De Niro).

As the film reaches its gradual denouement, the pressure builds, and there are some really memorable scenes. It looks great, it sounds great and the performances are excellent. It's a sweaty, sad, cerebral near-masterpiece.

50 MUST-SEE HORROR MOVIES

"Mephistopheles is such a mouthful in Manhattan, Johnny."

— Louis Cyphre

29) Near Dark, 1987
Director: Kathryn Bigelow
Runtime: 95 mins
Scare factor: 3/5

Not many horror films are directed by women, and *Near Dark* is by Oscar-winning Kathryn *Hurt Locker* Bigelow. The movie is more or less a love story meets Western meets vampires, and is all the better for it, working many of each genre's strong points into a decent whole.

Caleb Colton (Adrian Pasdar) is bitten by a vampire and joins their gang, but not wishing to kill to survive, he does not really fit in. There's some major twists at the end, and it – mostly – ends happily ever after (depending on who you were rooting for). A flop at the time, *Near Dark* has grown on fans and critics alike, and is justifiably well-regarded today.

50 MUST-SEE HORROR MOVIES

"Normal folks, they don't spit out bullets when you shoot 'em, no sir."

— Loy Colton

HORROR MOVIES

"[Chucky] says Aunt Maggie was a bitch and got what she deserved."

— Andy Barclay

㉚ Child's Play, 1988
Director: Tom Holland
Runtime: 87 mins
Scare factor: 2/5

Does humour belong in horror? There's nothing funny about this toy… A nasty serial killer's life force is transferred to a Good Guy talking doll that ends up in the hands of widow Karen Barclay (Catherine Hicks), then her son Andy (Alex Vincent). The doll, "Chucky", picks up where the human left off and goes on a murderous spree for which poor Andy takes the blame. You won't be surprised to hear that it doesn't end well for the doll.

Child's Play is a nasty movie that struck a chord with audiences, and Chucky himself takes a place in the pantheon of horror greats. And if you think this one's beyond the pail – using a child's plaything to scare people senseless – just wait until you get to 1998's *Bride of Chucky*.

HORROR MOVIES

"Sometimes I imagine she's alive. Somewhere far away. She's very happy."

— Rex Hofman

㉛ The Vanishing, 1988
Director: George Sluizer
Runtime: 107 mins
Scare factor: 3/5

There are no jump scares, shocks or gore in this European masterpiece on how to build a subtle, unnerving mystery. Rex (Gene Bervoets) and his girlfriend Saskia (Johanna ter Steege) are on holiday in France when she goes missing after walking into a motorway service station. Rex searches for her for years, eventually finding her kidnapper, who offers to show him exactly what happened to his girlfriend.

The movie is subtly filmed, the soundtrack menacing and the tension builds brilliantly, making for a very uneasy watch. And it'll make you think twice about nipping out to fetch something from a garage next time you're filling up.

HORROR MOVIES

㉜ Misery, 1990
Director: Rob Reiner
Runtime: 107 mins
Scare factor: 3/5

Once again, Stephen King hits all the right notes with an unnerving story. Rob Reiner directed this big-budget feature, a popular and critical success, which gave the world a new monster – for once female.

Writer Paul Sheldon (James Caan) crashes his car in the snow and is rescued by superfan Annie Wilkes (Kathy Bates). But when she finds out he is killing off her favourite character from his books, she takes matters into her own hands...

Featuring one of mainstream cinema's most unforgettable "turn-away" scenes, *Misery* is a claustrophobic, slow-burn tale of obsession and trauma. Caan is excellent as the writer, and Kathy Bates scooped a well-deserved Oscar for her performance as the increasingly deranged Wilkes.

50 MUST-SEE HORROR MOVIES

"I'm your number one fan. There's nothing to worry about. You're going to be just fine."

— Annie Wilkes

33. The Silence of the Lambs, 1991
Director: Jonathan Demme
Runtime: 118 mins
Scare factor: 4/5

Back in the day, this movie was HUGE. Thrilling, graphic, nasty and above all genuinely disturbing, *The Silence of the Lambs* was the biggest big-hit serial-killer movie of them all. Clarice Starling (Jodie Foster) is a young FBI trainee who is tasked with getting serial killer Hannibal Lecter (Anthony Hopkins) to help on another case. He does so, but at a cost. It goes about as well as you would expect and ends with what has become one of the most famous lines in cinematic history.

Plenty of tense scenes and a finale that will have you screaming on the edge of the sofa, *The Silence of the Lambs* is everything it is said to be.

50 MUST-SEE HORROR MOVIES

"It rubs the lotion on its skin. It does this whenever it is told."

— **Buffalo Bill**

34. Candyman, 1992
Director: Bernard Rose
Runtime: 101 mins
Scare factor: 3/5

Candyman is notable for a few reasons: it's a Black horror film; it's been a huge influence on subsequent generations of filmmakers; and it's a damn fine, scary piece of cinema. Written and directed by Bernard Rose, it is based on the short story by Clive Barker.

Helen Lyle (Virginia Madsen) is a student who is researching urban legends, including the story of Candyman, a former slave whose spirit returns to kill anyone who speaks his name before a mirror. Before you can say, well, "Candyman", Helen has spoken the name five times, seemingly to no effect. You won't be surprised to hear that it all goes downhill, and murder, mystery and plenty of blood follow. The folklore and slavery storylines give the movie an even more disturbing dimension, in a country that has never really dealt with its past. *Candyman* is gripping, terrifying and eminently watchable.

"They will say that I have shed innocent blood. What's blood for if not for shedding?"

— Candyman

HORROR MOVIES

"No, please don't kill me, Mr Ghostface, I wanna be in the sequel!"

— Tatum

35) Scream, 1996
Director: Wes Craven
Runtime: 111 mins
Scare factor: 3/5

Scream (see page 6) ushered in yet another new era of teen slasher movies. But if anyone knows how to work a cinema and have the audience petrified time after time it is Wes Craven, and on that front *Scream* does not disappoint.

Made with a knowing eye, and mocking previous teen-horror tropes, *Scream* was a roaring success, re-establishing Craven's credentials, boosting a new generation of young American actors, and making plenty of money in the process. It's the usual story – unwitting teens and a horrible history – but the meta-humour and self-acknowledgement make this a wholly original piece of cinema. If only they'd patented the mask.

HORROR MOVIES

㊱ Ringu (Ring), 1998
Director: Hideo Nakata
Runtime: 95 mins
Scare factor: 4/5

There was certainly Japanese horror prior to *Ring*, but it was by no means mainstream. This movie was the start of a stream of Asian films, some of which proved to be hugely influential on the horror genre as a whole. In *Ring*, urban legend tells of a video tape that, once watched, will cause the death of the viewer, after a mysterious follow-up telephone call. Reiko (Nanako Matsushima) is a reporter investigating the death of her niece and other high-school students. This leads her on a voyage of dark discovery to the source of a curse... and a way to prevent it.

Ring is thrilling, well-paced and mysterious, creepy not gory, and will linger long in the mind. NB: the original is much better than the remake, although that is also worth a watch.

50 MUST-SEE HORROR MOVIES

> "This kind of thing... it doesn't start by one person telling a story. It's more like everyone's fear just takes on a life of its own."
>
> — Ryuji Takayama

HORROR MOVIES

㊲ The Blair Witch Project, 1999
Directors: Daniel Myrick, Eduardo Sánchez
Runtime: 81 mins
Scare factor: 4/5

An independent, low-budget movie that hit the jackpot, *The Blair Witch Project* changed the face of horror movies. Purporting to be a "found-footage" movie made by three college students in Maryland, the entire film is made up of handheld, documentary-style accounts of a journey the students make; they don't come back.

No monsters (well, none that you see anyway), scant gore and very little explanation means the viewer is left to put the pieces together themselves. A huge hit and one of the most profitable horror films of all time, *The Blair Witch Project* paved the way for other successes of this type, such as *Cloverfield* and *Paranormal Activity*.

50 MUST-SEE HORROR MOVIES

"OK, here's your motivation. You're lost, you're angry in the woods, and no one is here to help you."

— Josh Leonard

HORROR MOVIES

㊳ The Sixth Sense, 1999
Director: M. Night Shyamalan
Runtime: 108 mins
Scare factor: 4/5

A study in how to make someone feel uneasy for 108 minutes, *The Sixth Sense* is a neatly paced thriller/horror/ghost story. Malcolm Crowe (Bruce Willis), a child psychologist, is shot by one of his former patients. A few months later, he starts seeing Cole Sear (Haley Joel Osment), a child suffering from symptoms reminiscent of the patient that shot Crowe.

The film was a huge success, and the twist at the end is still brilliantly done, assuming you can avoid knowledge of it before you see the film. Willis and Osment work really well together and this was M. Night Shyamalan's big breakthrough – by no means the last.

50 MUST-SEE HORROR MOVIES

"I know what I want: I want to be able to talk to my wife again. The way we used to talk to each other."

— Malcolm

㊴ Audition, 1999
Director: Takashi Miike
Runtime: 113 mins
Scare factor: 6/5

A graphic exploration of relationships that pushes the boundaries of taste and entertainment, *Audition* is a story of love and loss, albeit one that involves torture, murder and severed body parts.

Shigeharu Aoyama's (Ryo Ishibashi) wife dies and he is encouraged to meet someone else by his son, Shigehiko (Tetsu Sawaki). The former ends up holding auditions for a fake movie but, in fact, the part on offer is that of his new wife. He is intrigued by one of the women who tries for the role, Asami (Eihi Shiina), and they develop a relationship. The story slowly unravels to some very nasty reveals, and culminates in an extremely graphic torture scene that once viewed is never forgotten. *Audition* is a very good film that has influenced many since, but is not for the faint-hearted.

50 MUST-SEE HORROR MOVIES

"Only pain and suffering will make you realize who you are."

— Asami

HORROR MOVIES

"We fight off the infected or we wait until they starve to death, and then what?"

— Major Henry West

㊽ 28 Days Later, 2002
Director: Danny Boyle
Runtime: 113 mins
Scare factor: 3/5

In many ways the bastard, undead love-child of *Night of the Living Dead* and *The Day of the Triffids* (if there could be such a thing), *28 Days Later* is superb. Tense, exciting and powerful, the loneliness and drama of surviving a zombie apocalypse becomes all too believable.

Cycle courier Jim (Cillian Murphy) wakes up in hospital to find himself alone. He eventually meets other survivors of what turns out to be a horrific virus (sound familiar?) that has wiped out most of the population. The opening scenes, of a deserted, post-catastrophe London, are particularly strong, and the pace speeds up as much dramatic nastiness ensues. An absolute classic.

HORROR MOVIES

"Hello... Adam, Doctor Gordon. I want to play a game."

— John Kramer/Jigsaw

(41) Saw, 2004
Director: James Wan
Runtime: 103 mins
Scare factor: 5/5

The low-budget movie *Saw* ushered in a new dawn of graphic, dilemma-heavy horror. Some "saw" it as little more than a long series of sadistic games and bloody violence, but for others it was a pulsing, exciting, mysterious and highly original movie.

Two men (Leigh Whannell and Cary Elwes) awaken in a dirty bathroom. There's a dead body between them. One is informed that if he kills the other (they're chained to opposite sides of the room) using the gun (in the corpse's hand), his wife and daughter won't be murdered: it's nasty. With its dominant self-mutilation tropes, *Saw* is a horrible film, although the voyeur theme works really well in horror.

HORROR MOVIES

㊷ El Orfanato (The Orphanage), 2007
Director: J.A. Bayona
Runtime: 97 mins
Scare factor: 3/5

More disturbing than scary, although there are a few jumpy moments, *The Orphanage* slowly reveals the tragic events that passed in an institution.

Laura (Belén Rueda) grew up in said orphanage and revisits it as an adult, with the plan of reopening it. She is accompanied by her husband Carlos (Fernando Cayo) and adopted son Simón (Roger Príncep). The latter goes missing after meeting an imaginary friend and there are plenty of scary events and shocking revelations. A haunting story (literally), *The Orphanage* eschews shock for subtlety with superb effect – and it is certainly creepy.

50 MUST-SEE HORROR MOVIES

"Seeing is not believing. It's the other way around. Believe, and you will see."

— Aurora

HORROR MOVIES

㊸ Låt den rätte komma in (Let the Right One In), 2008
Director: Tomas Alfredson
Runtime: 114 mins
Scare factor: 3/5

Let the Right One In is a very original take on vampires. More a coming-of-age story involving young people and their relationships with the outside world, there is plenty of vampire naughtiness and blood spilled (and sprayed).

Eli (Lina Leandersson) moves into the apartment next door to Oskar (Kåre Hedebrant), a boy who is being bullied. To find out how this becomes a vampire story – with all the associated violence, murder and blood – you'll just have to watch it. Horror films from Sweden are rare, but this is one of the best: a shocking tale that transcends the genre.

50 MUST-SEE HORROR MOVIES

"I'm twelve. But I've been twelve for a long time."

— Eli

HORROR MOVIES

㊹ The Babadook, 2014
Director: Jennifer Kent
Runtime: 94 mins
Scare factor: 4/5

Australia is not famed for its horror offerings (sorry, Peter Jackson's *Bad Taste*), but 2014's *The Babadook* goes some way to correct the balance. Amelia (Essie Davis) and Samuel (Noah Wiseman) live in Adelaide following the death of Amelia's husband while she was in labour with Samuel. She reads her son a pop-up book, *Mister Babadook*, about a monster that he believes is real. Plenty of nasty stuff follows (murder, demonic possession, haunting – the usual), but the movie is well-paced and features many memorable, albeit disturbing, scenes.

You'd just better hope nobody knocks on your door with "three sharp knocks" while you're watching this one.

50 MUST-SEE HORROR MOVIES

"It's just a book. It can't hurt you."

— Amelia

HORROR MOVIES

"Are you a good boy?"

— The girl

㊹ A Girl Walks Home Alone at Night, 2014
Director: Ana Lily Amirpour
Runtime: 101 mins
Scare factor: 2/5

One of few foreign-language films in this list, *AGWHAaN* may well be the only Iranian-Western-vampire-horror movie you'll ever see (2016's *Under the Shadow* is another must-watch). It's not really like anything else, and it has a haunting, other-worldly atmosphere.

It is ostensibly the story of Arash, a young Iranian man with a drug-addicted father in Bad City. There's plenty more, including a skateboarding vampire, a drug-influenced party scene and an impromptu piercing session, all accompanied by a superb soundtrack. A commentary on many things other than vampires, *A Girl Walks Home Alone at Night* is ultimately a brilliant, moody movie.

HORROR MOVIES

㊻ Train to Busan, 2016
Director: Yeon Sang-ho
Runtime: 118 mins
Scare factor: 3/5

Like a cross between *The Walking Dead* and *Runaway Train*, the South Korean *Train to Busan* is a slick, scary, fast-paced, thrilling zombie movie. Workaholic Seok-woo (Gong Yoo) attempts to make amends with his daughter (Kim Su-an) by taking her to Busan on a fast train. Unfortunately for them (and everyone else on the train), they happen to time this with the last-second arrival of a young woman who is infected with a deadly zombie virus, and who proceeds to pass it on. It's a race against time to get to the safe zone...

A superb zombie flick with a clever core, *Train to Busan* was a worldwide hit.

50 MUST-SEE HORROR MOVIES

"Sorry, but you're infected."

— Seok-woo

HORROR MOVIES

㊽ Get Out, 2017
Director: Jordan Peele
Runtime: 104 mins
Scare factor: 3/5

The best horror films use the genre as a device to encourage an audience to reflect on how we function as a society, asking unpleasant questions at the same time. *Get Out* does just that, using racism in America to make a movie that's scary on many levels. Chris Washington (Daniel Kaluuya) goes to meet his (white) girlfriend's (Allison Williams) parents in upstate New York. They have Black servants, and at a party, Chris has some very odd interactions.

Get Out is a simply brilliant movie, making most viewers very uncomfortable and asking pertinent questions about society and prejudices: essential viewing.

50 MUST-SEE HORROR MOVIES

"Chris, you gotta get the fuck up outta there, man! You in some *Eyes Wide Shut* situation."

— Rod

48. Hereditary, 2018
Director: Ari Aster
Runtime: 127 mins
Scare factor: 3/5

Families can cause you all sorts of problems, right? When it comes to *Hereditary*, you ain't seen nothing yet... It's an original movie, which runs at an odd pace, and includes tropes from all manner of genres as it takes the viewer on a choppy ride around a somewhat dysfunctional family and their odd past (and present).

It is beautifully filmed, the cast is superb and the setting is extremely clever. Even the soundtrack is great. *Hereditary* is filled with memorable moments and plenty of surprises – a marvellous film that's well worth a watch.

50 MUST-SEE HORROR MOVIES

"I never wanted to be your mother."

— Annie

HORROR MOVIES

"Let's make some traps or something, like some *Home Alone* type stuff."

— Gabe

㊾ Us, 2019
Director: Jordan Peele
Runtime: 116 mins
Scare factor: 4/5

What Jordan Peele started in *Get Out*, he continues here. Another film that's superficially a horror about a regular family, below the surface it's a disconcerting discussion of identity, race and place in modern America.

Adelaide Thomas (Lupita Nyong'o) has an odd experience as a child, encountering her double in a fun house. Years later, her family is attacked by four people who look exactly like them... *Us* is brilliant, fast-paced and exciting. But it's also deeply thought-provoking, asking extremely pertinent questions about contemporary society and modern American history.

50. Midsommar, 2019
Director: Ari Aster
Runtime: 147 mins
Scare factor: 4/5

Sweden's reputation is that it is full of peaceful, calm people who celebrate the seasons and are at one with nature. *Midsommar* offers another view...

Christian (Jack Reynor) is an American student who is invited to a special midsummer festival with his friends. They attend, but events get increasingly more bizarre and unsettling. The festival ends in human sacrifice and disturbing rituals, with plenty of blood and misery on the way. *Midsommar* will probably have you crossing a June visit to Sweden off your bucket list.

50 MUST-SEE HORROR MOVIES

"That's cultural, you know? We stick our elders in nursing homes. I'm sure they find that disturbing."

— Christian

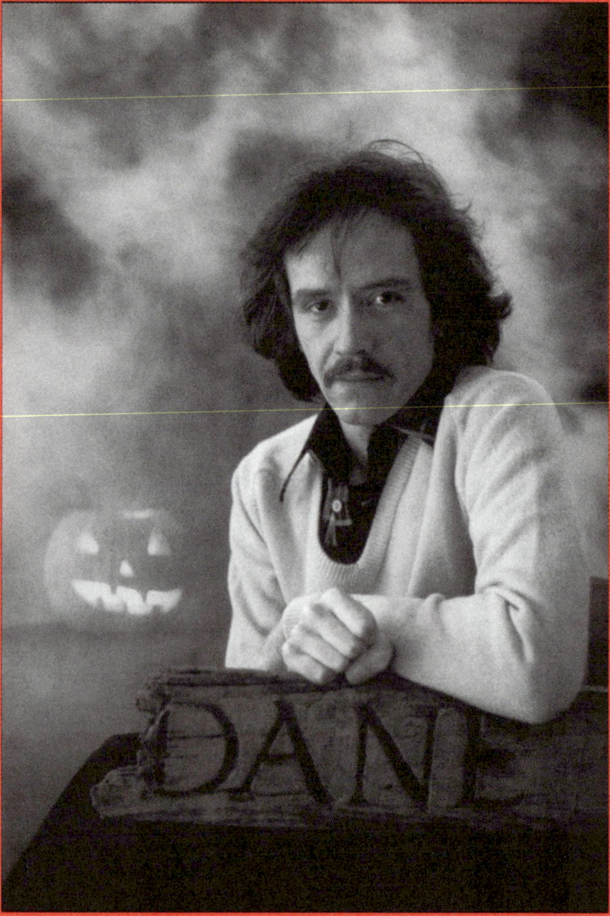
DAN

★ ★ ★ ★ ★

DIRECTORS' CUT

HORROR MOVIES

Roman Polanski (1933–)

Polanski was born in Paris, and is a French-Polish film director, producer and screenwriter whose seminal films include *Chinatown*, 1974, as well as *Rosemary's Baby*, 1968. He is the recipient of numerous accolades, including, in 2003, winning Best Director Oscar for *The Pianist*, 2002. His work focuses on a variety of genres, exploring themes of isolation, desire and absurdity.

Tobe Hooper (1943–2017)

Born in Austin, Texas, Hooper was an American filmmaker who was best known for his horror movies, and cited by the British Film Institute as the most influential in this genre. Beginning as a documentary cameraman, he rose to fame when he joined up with Kim Henkel to make *The Texas Chain Saw Massacre*, 1974, which not only landed him in Hollywood but also changed the horror-film industry when it became an instant classic.

George A. Romero (1940–2017)

An American-Canadian film director, writer, editor and actor, Romero was born in The Bronx, New York, and died in Toronto. His *Night of the Living Dead* series of films about a zombie apocalypse is considered a major contributor to the horror genre in filmmaking and the image of the zombie in modern culture. Working with makeup and special-effects artist, Tom Savini, the films secured him a place in horror history. He achieved immense success in the 1970s and 1980s with more blockbuster films such as *Creepshow* in 1982.

DIRECTORS' CUT

"We had $6,000 and a loose idea... an allegorical thing. We decided to take that and turn it into a real blood and guts film, and that's how it started."

— George A. Romero on *Night of the Living Dead*, *Filmmakers Newsletter Magazine*, 1972

John Carpenter (1948–)

Carpenter (see page 118) is an American filmmaker, composer and actor who was born in Carthage, New York. He is most commonly associated with horror, action and science films of the 1970s and 1980s, which earned him the titles "Master of Horror" and "Prince of Darkness". *Halloween*, 1978, brought great commercial success and helped to develop the slasher genre, as well as featuring his work as a composer with the "Halloween Theme", which became recognizable in its own right.

DIRECTORS' CUT

Wes Craven (1939—2015)

Craven was born in Cleveland, Ohio, and died in Los Angeles, California. A prolific film director, screenwriter and producer, he worked primarily in the horror genre, particularly with slasher films that notably mixed horror cliches with humour. Recognized as one of the great masters in his field, his contributions to the hall of fame include the spectre of Freddy Krueger (played by actor Robert Englund) and Ghostface (voiced by Roger L. Jackson). His films often had an underlying reference to social inequalities and the decline of the family, but with nightmarish trappings.

Jordan Peele (1979–)

Peele is an American actor, comedian and filmmaker who was born in New York City. He is best known for his work in film and television in the comedy and horror genres. He has received various accolades and in 2017 he was included on the annual TIME100 list of the most influential people in the world. After becoming well known in early comic sketches such as *Mad TV* and *Key & Peele*, he made his directorial debut with the horror film *Get Out*, 2017, and went on to later success with many other film and television projects.

DIRECTORS' CUT

Ari Aster (1986–)

Aster is an American filmmaker who was born in New York. Beginning his craft with short films, he made his feature debut *Hereditary* in 2018 to critical acclaim. Staring Toni Collette and Gabriel Byrne, the horror tale was a huge hit and he soon followed with psychological thriller *Midsommar* in 2019, which also featured an impressive cast including Florence Pugh and Will Poulter. His next film, *Beau is Afraid*, came out in 2023.

HORROR MOVIES

"I'm scared to close my eyes, I'm scared to open them! We're gonna die out here!"

— Heather Donahue,
The Blair Witch Project, **1999**